Simon Bor

Simon, along with his partner Sara, is a multi-award winning children's animation producer of over twenty series for television. Projects include Tube Mice, Binka, Grizzly Tales for Gruesome Kids and Wolves, Witches & Giants which have been sold to over a hundred countries world wide.

He first discovered printmaking while a student at the Cambridge School of Art, and later at St Martin's School of Art. He studied Animation at West Surrey College of Art & Design in Farnham and set up Honeycomb Animation with Sara in the mid eighties. Returning to printmaking in 2011, he works from his own studio, as well as attending Mary Gillett's Dartmoor workshops. He is a member of the Double Elephant Print Workshop in Exeter.

Beyond animation and printmaking, Simon gained an MA in Professional Writing from Falmouth University in 2014 and published 'Red Riding Hood's Phone: Hacked' in 2015. His first book of prints, 'Cambridge Lost in Time' was published in 2016. He lives in the Devon countryside with Sara and his two daughters, Aimei and Anna.

simonbor.co.uk

Also by Simon Bor, available at amazon.co.uk

Cambridge Lost in Time: Prints by Simon Bor

Etchings, Woodcuts and Linocuts of some of Cambridge's lost buildings.

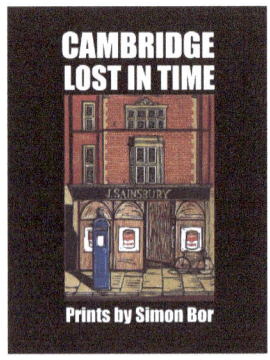

Red Riding Hood's Phone: Hacked

An illustrated retelling of the fairy tale using fictional social media. Also includes the short story, 'Loup Hall'.

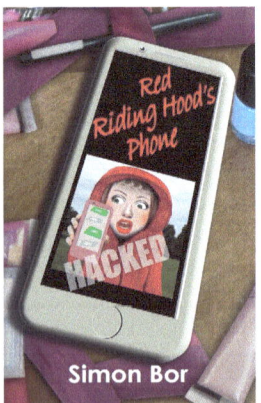

Water's Edge

Prints by Simon Bor

Water's Edge

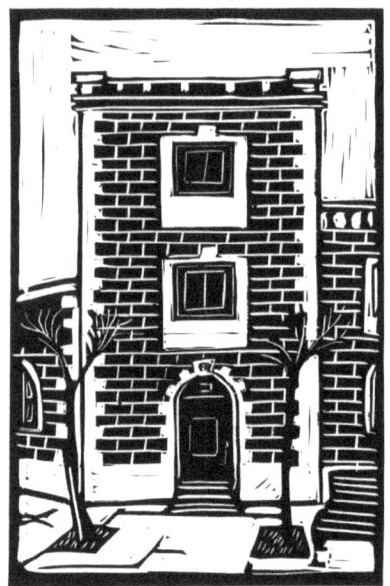 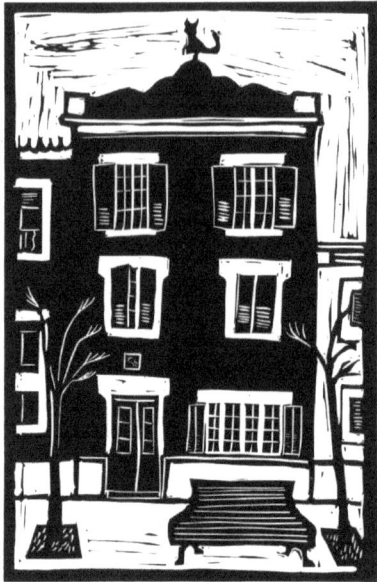 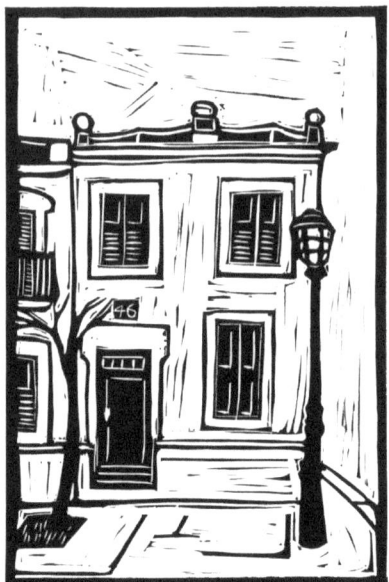

Cambridge	5
West Penwith and Devon	9
Menorca	21
London	19
Argyle	23

Cambridge

In this second collection of prints, my subject is not one particular place as it was in 'Cambridge Lost in Time'; it is where land meets sea, buildings meet rivers, man-made canals and mill leats.

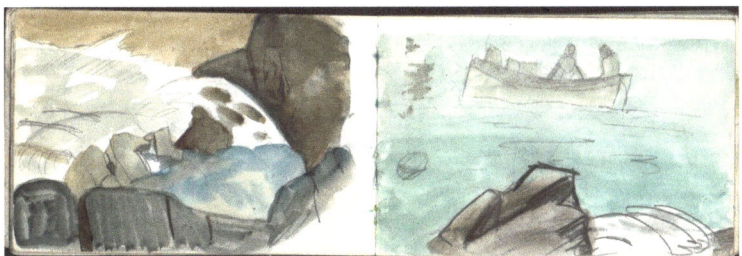

I've spent time at the water's edge, much of it with sketchbook and pencils at hand. Drawings I've made recently or decades ago have inspired much of my printmaking. I grew up by the sea in Wales, but it was Cambridge where I first discovered print at the Cambridge School of Art's print workshop at St Barnabas. I was very nearly banned from continuing to use the facilities as my prints of caricatures were not appreciated by tutor, Walter Hoyle. I was able to convince him that I was serious about printmaking by turning my attention to architectural lithographs.

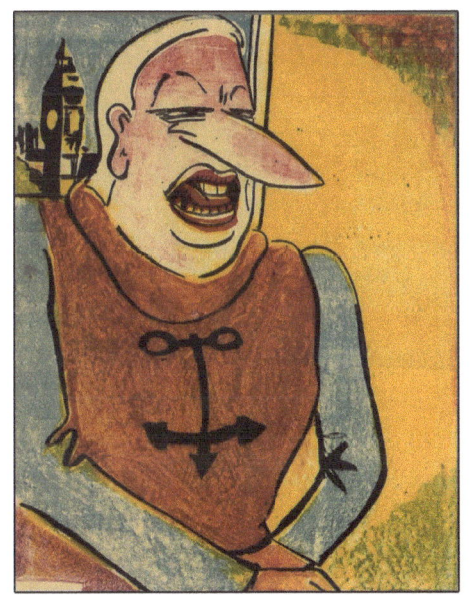
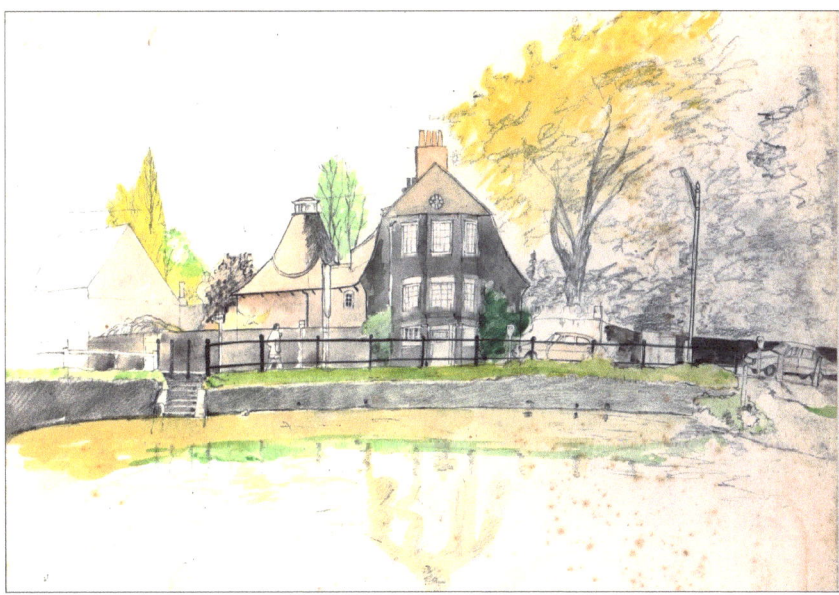

Above: a sketchbook from a 1977 return visit to Wales. Left: an early lithograph produced at the Cambridge School of Art. Right: the original sketch of The Mill Pond from 1976.

Water's Edge

The Mill Pond

Woodcut 2017

450 x 600 mm

Prints by Simon Bor

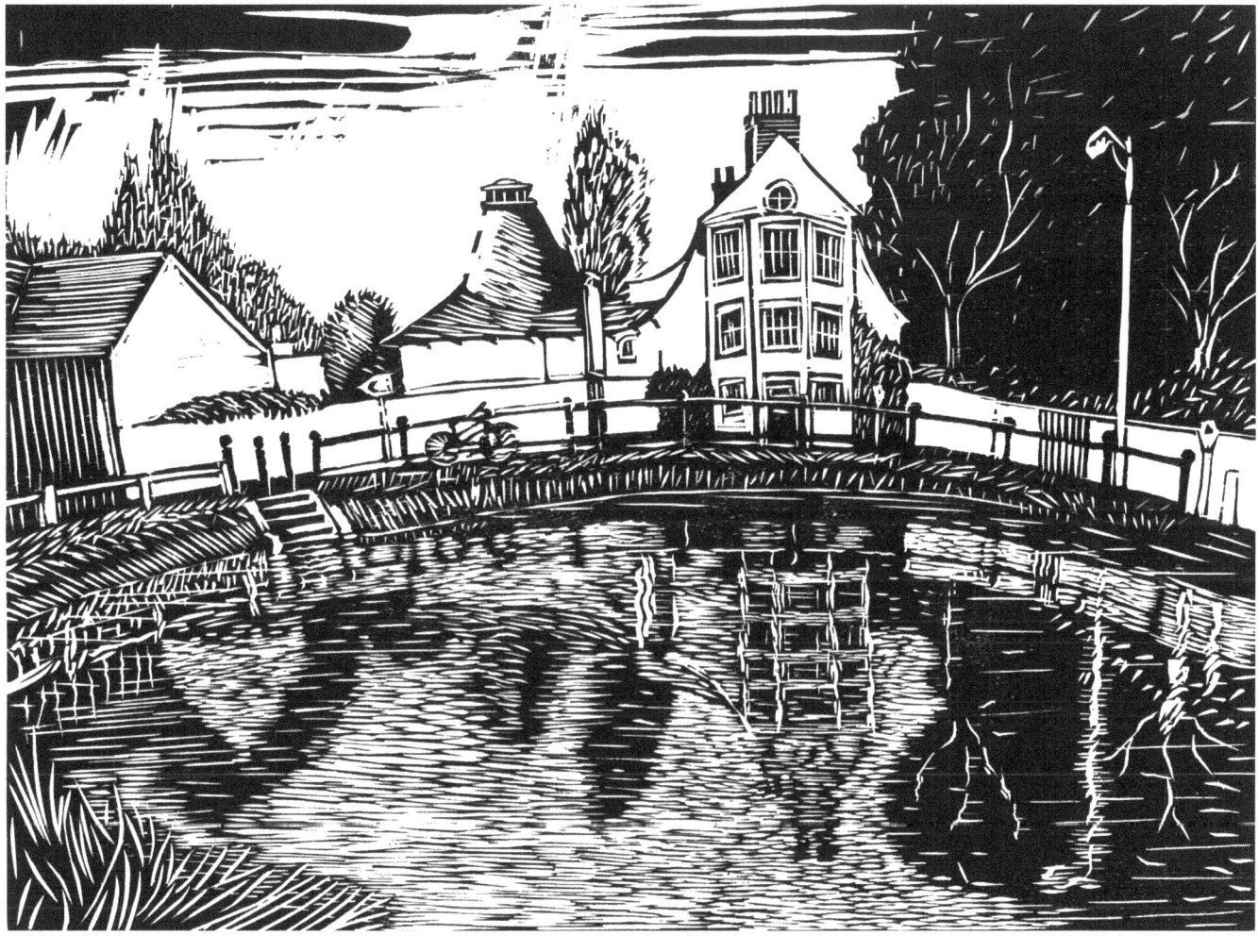

Water's Edge

West Penwith and Devon

My wife and I have lived in Devon since the late eighties and we were lucky enough to own a second home in Cornwall for a few years while our children were growing up; situated just a couple miles from Land's End, the area still inspires much of our work.

I discovered that the farm next door to us was used as a location set for an early Doctor Who serial with William Hartnell. 'The Smugglers' was the first time the BBC had ventured beyond the South East for filming. Other locations used included the nearby beach at Nanjizal.

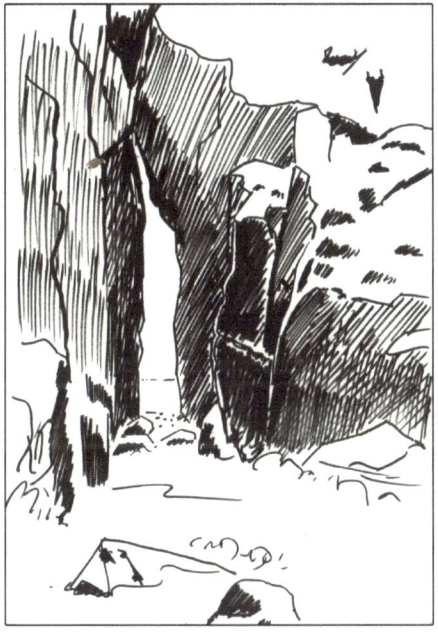 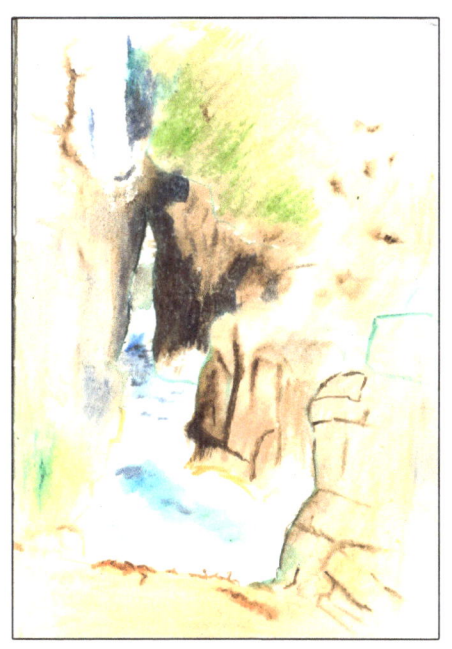

Studies for the Nanjizal print.

Water's Edge

Lamorna Cove

Collagraph and Linocut 2017

410 x 315mm

Prints by Simon Bor

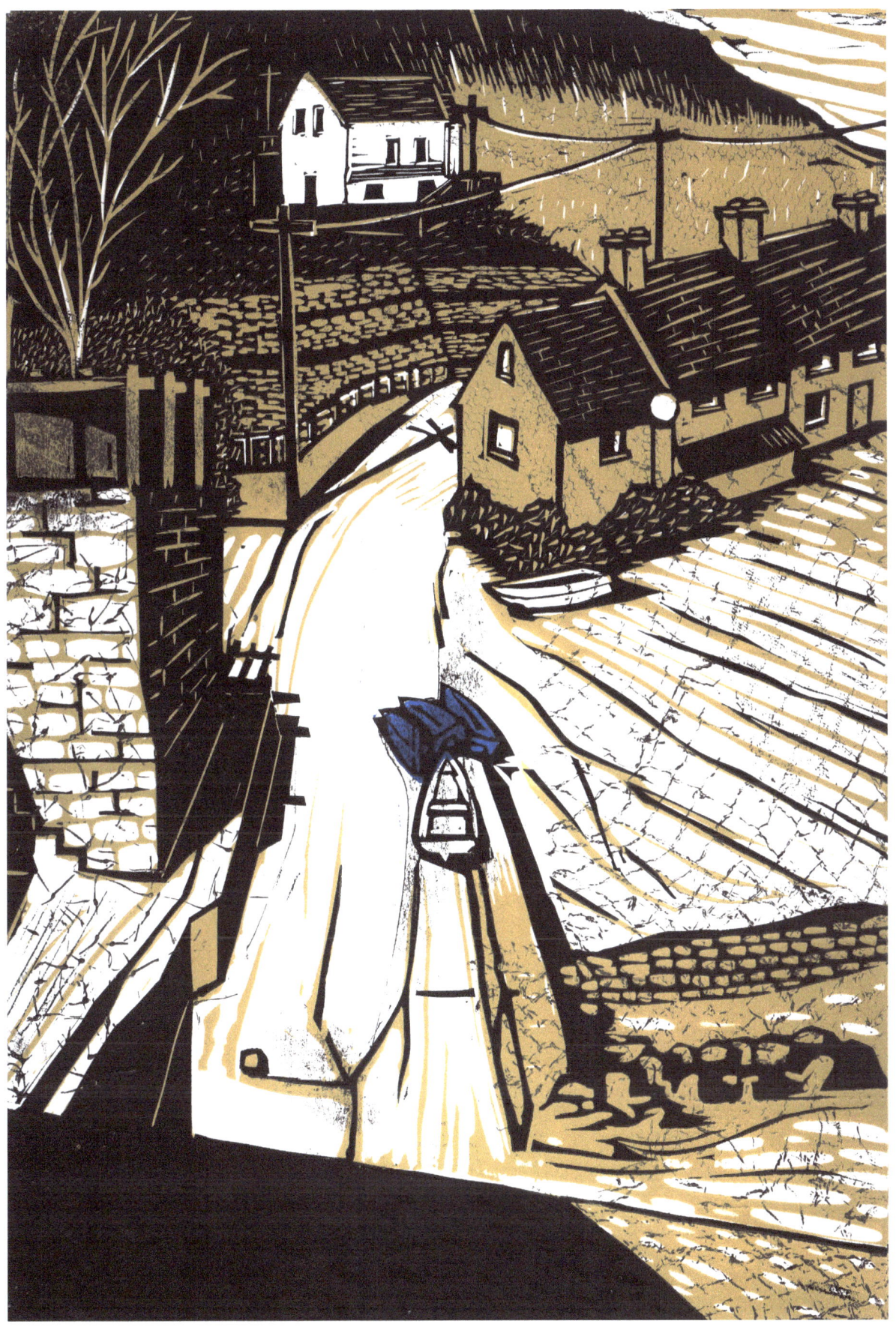

Water's Edge

Nanjizal: West Penwith

Linocut 2017

300 x 205 mm

Prints by Simon Bor

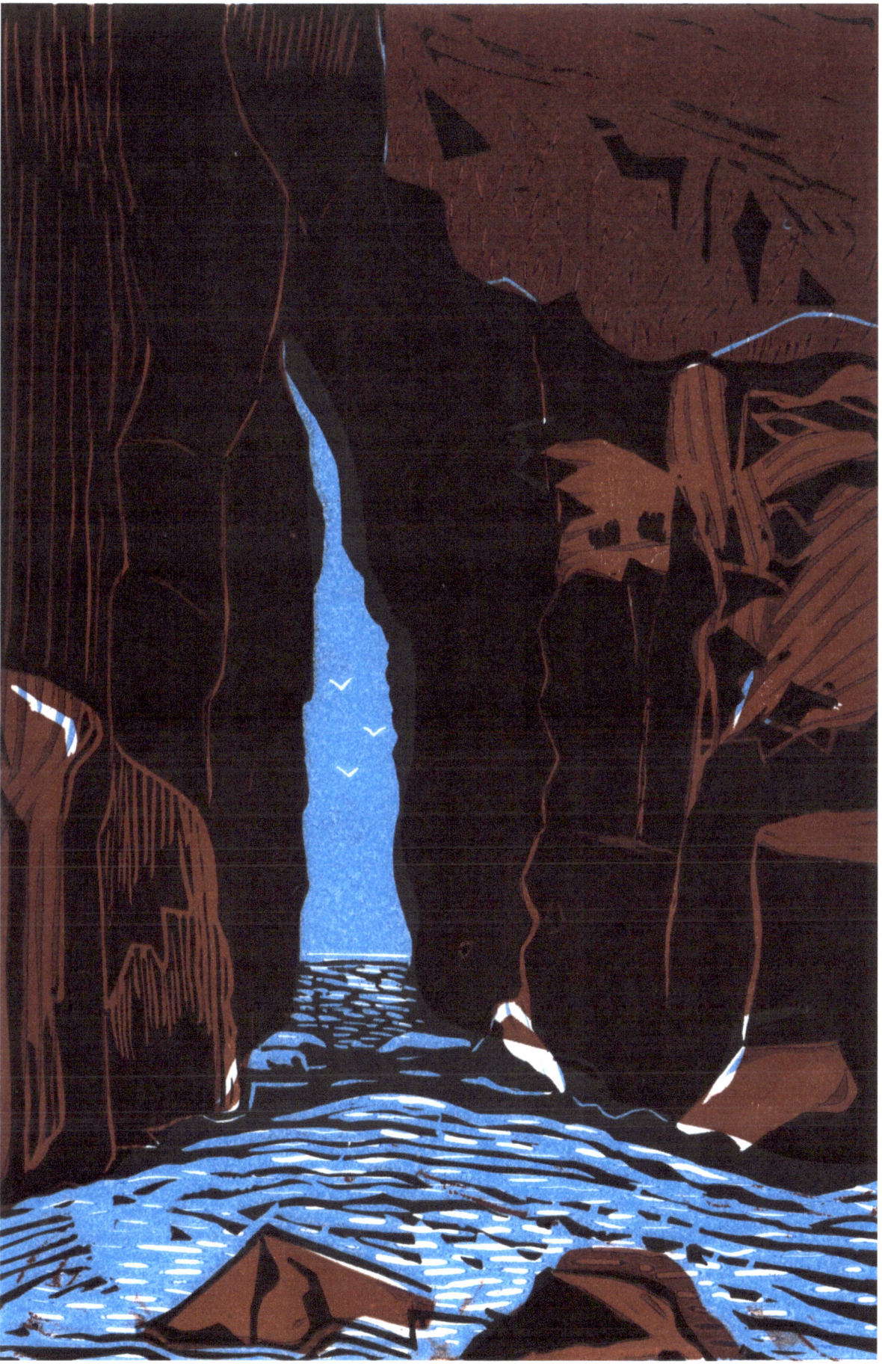

Water's Edge

Porth Chaple: Cornwall

Reduction woodcut 2017

450 mm x 300 mm

Prints by Simon Bor

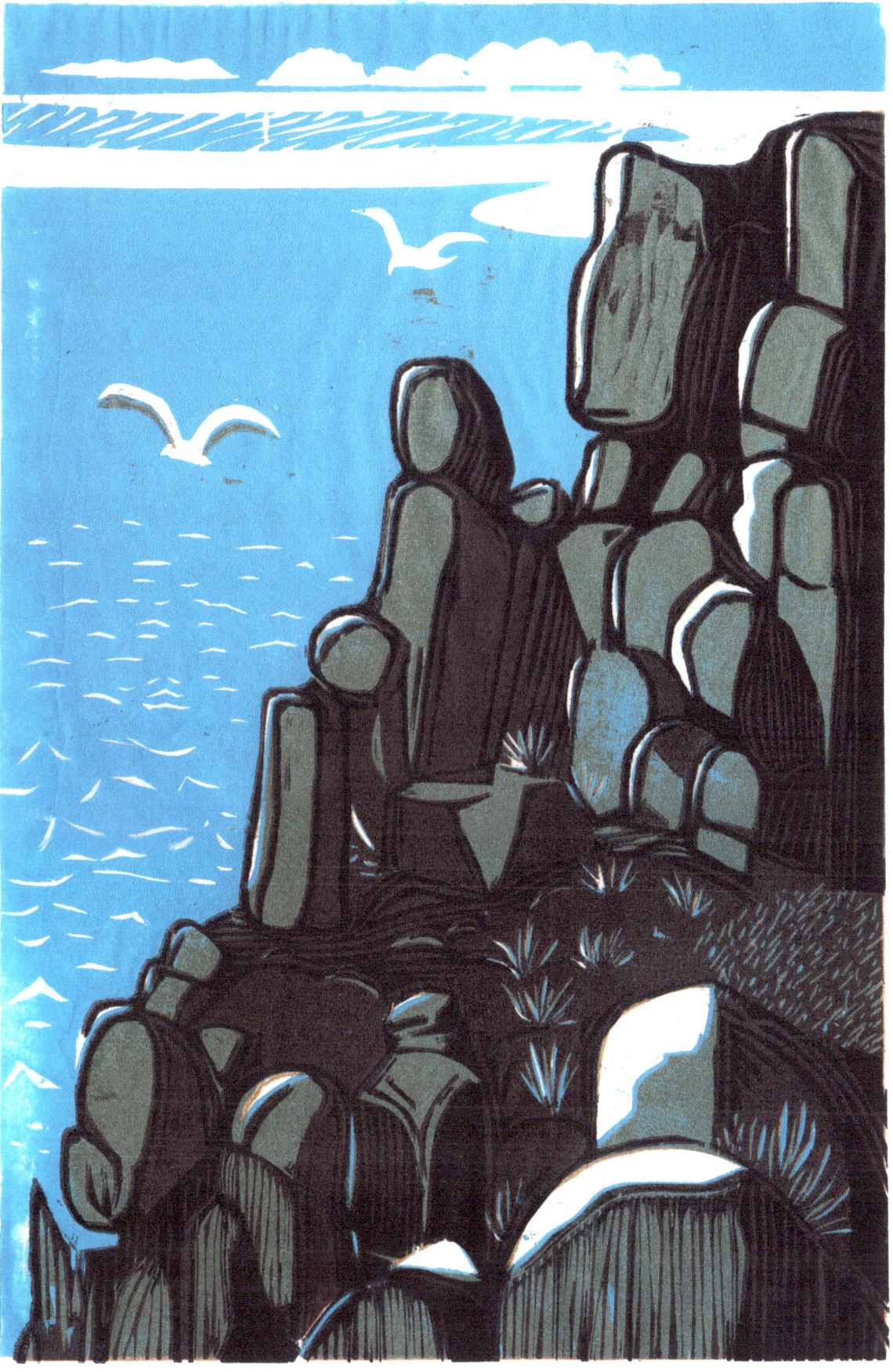

Water's Edge

The Old Gaol: Topsham

Photo Etching 2015

200 x 200 mm

Prints by Simon Bor

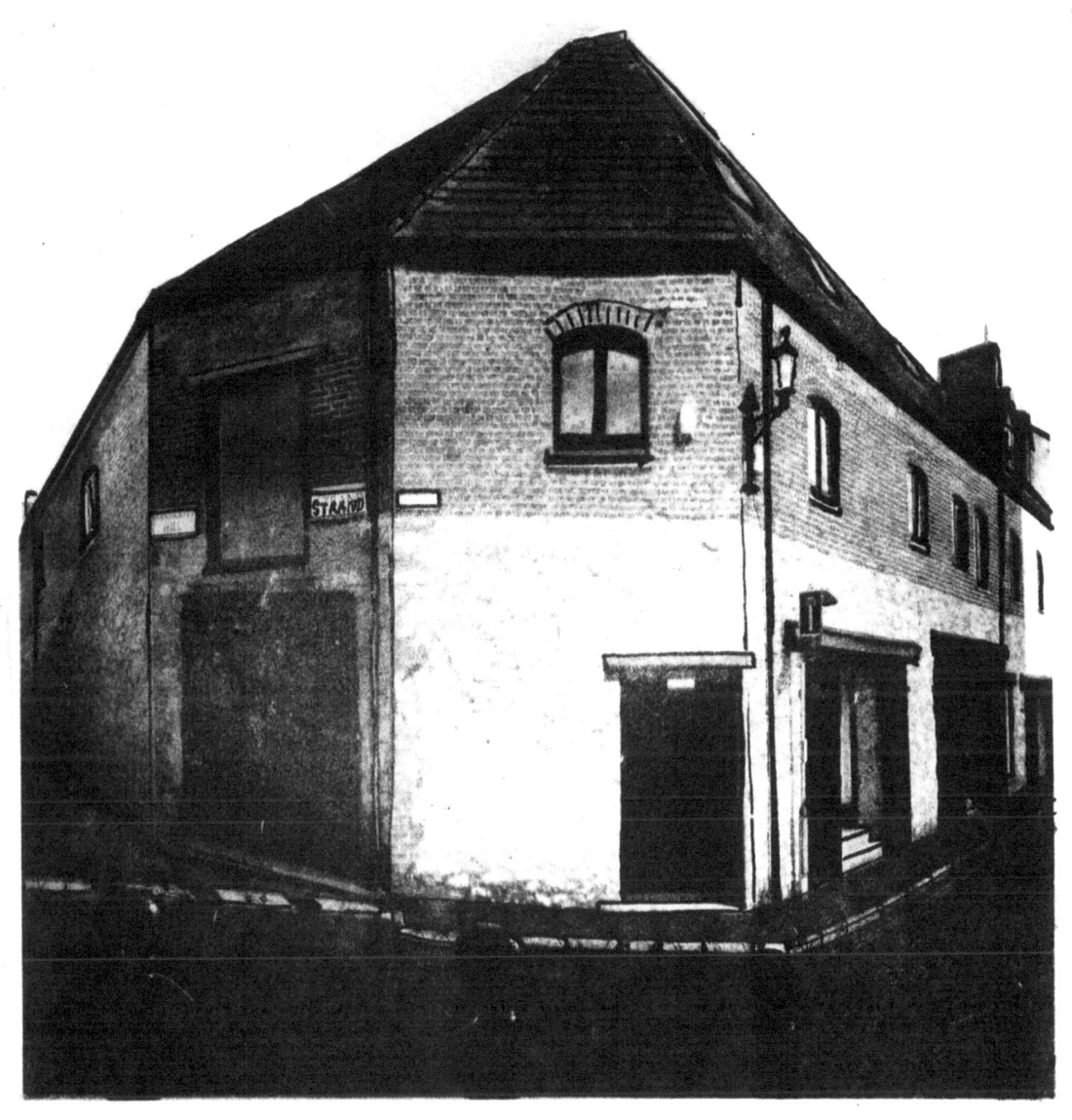

Water's Edge

Bickleigh-on-Exe

Monoprint and Linocut 2011

405 x 300 mm

Prints by Simon Bor

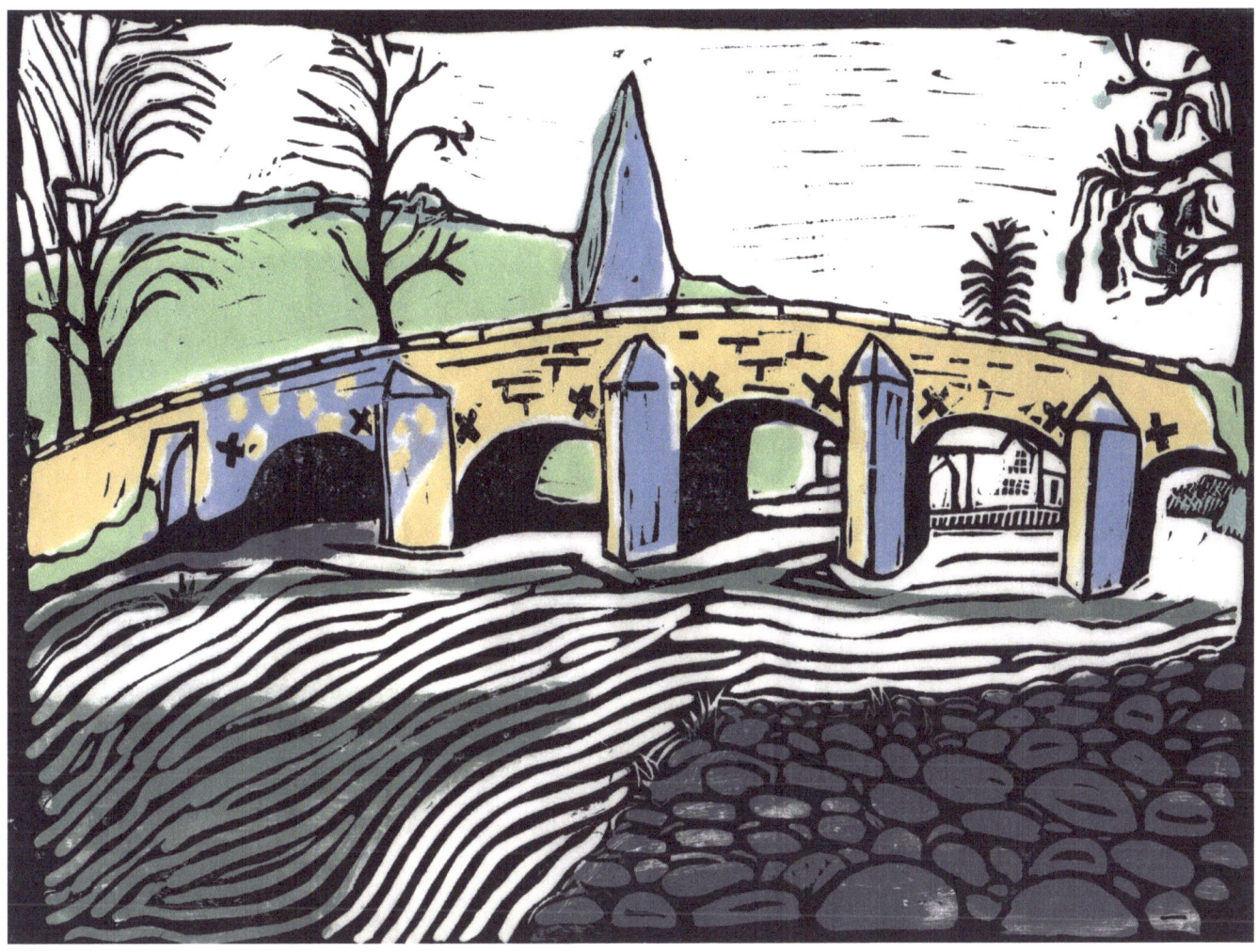

Water's Edge

Menorca

The sketchbook travels with me, as it did for two visits to the island of Menorca a few years ago. We stayed on the Carrer de Bellavista, Es Castell, which has a Georgian terrace overlooking the sea channel used by the big cruise ships in and out of the port of Mahón.

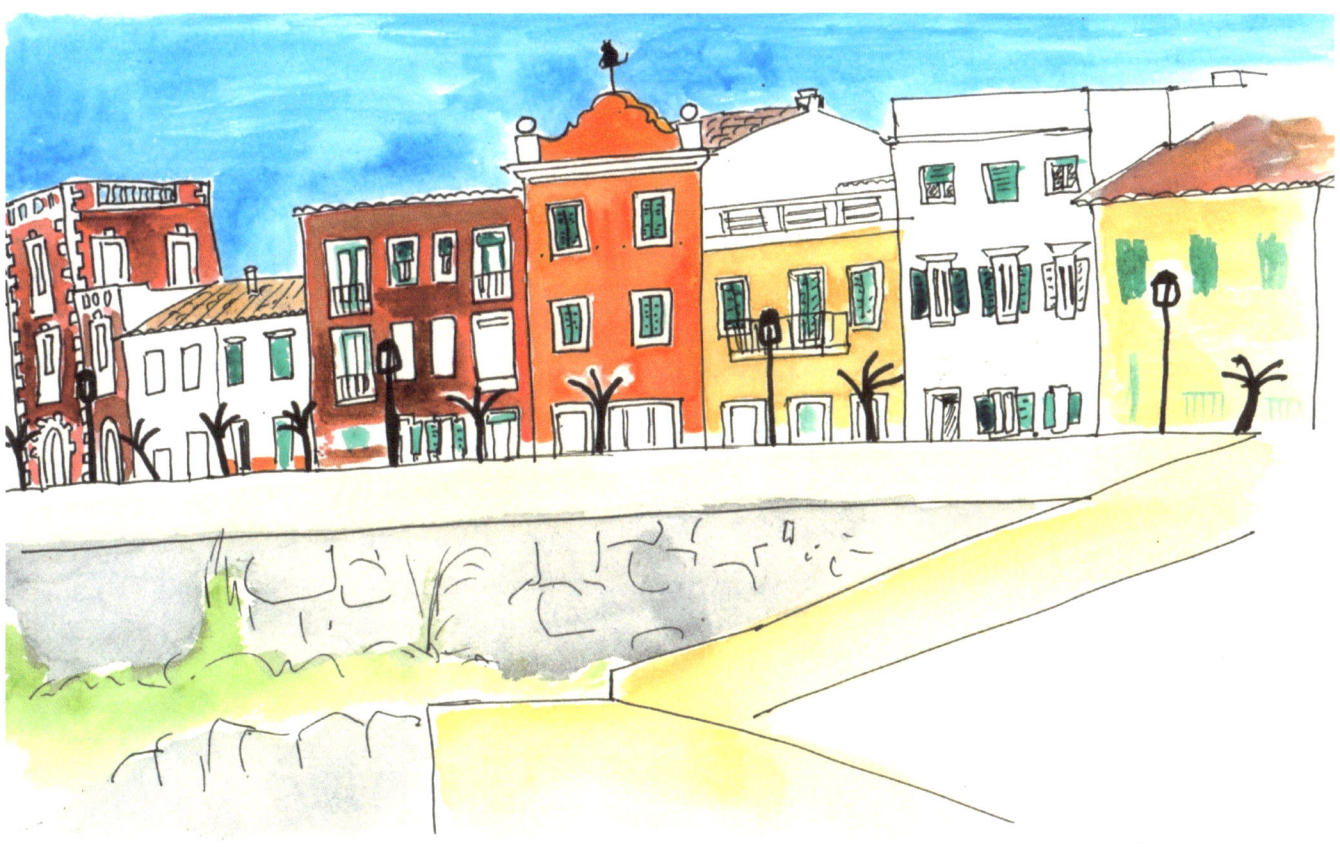

46 Carrer Bellavista

Linocut 2011

200 x 300 mm

Prints by Simon Bor

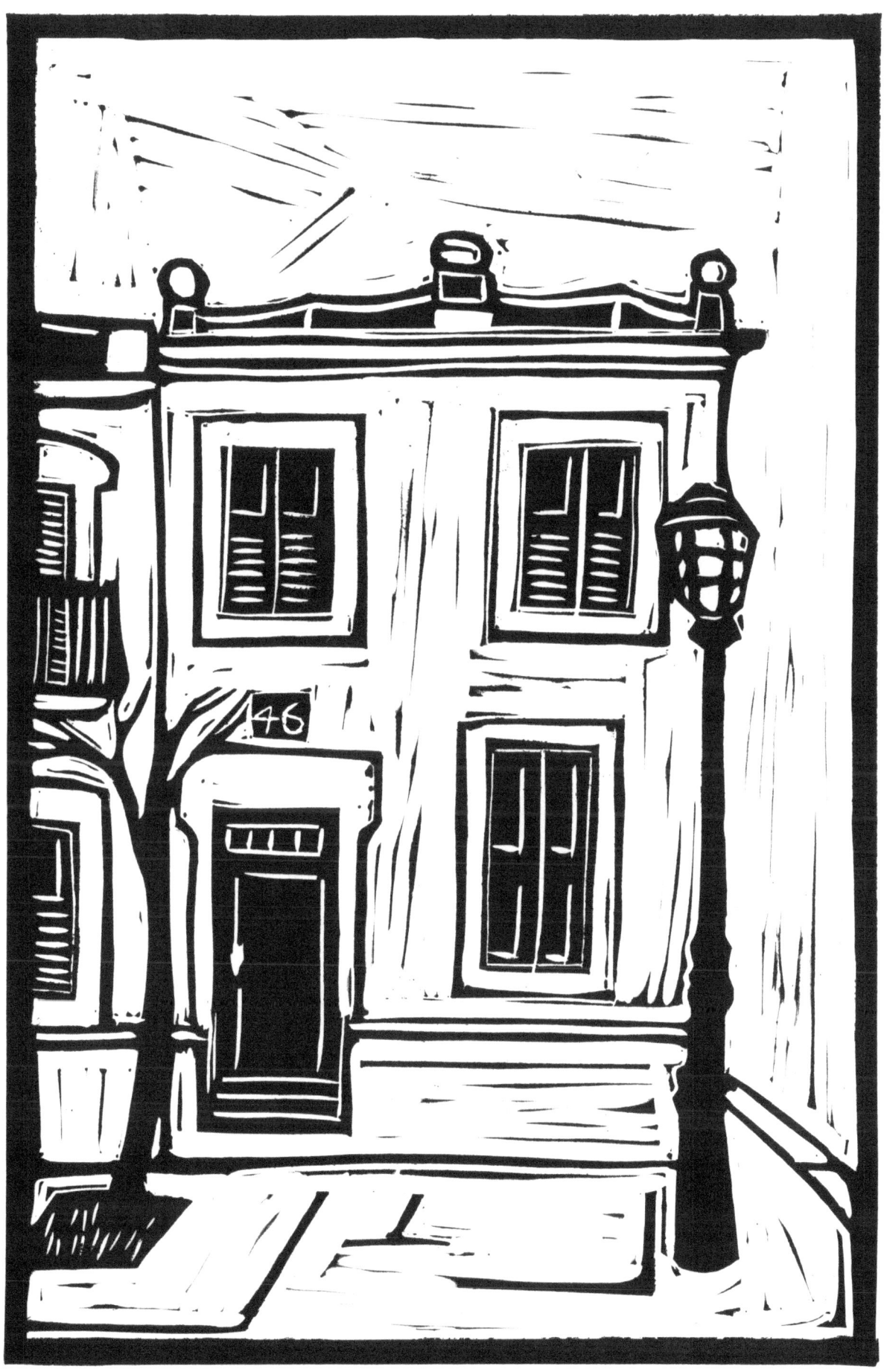

Water's Edge

56 Carrer Bellavista

Linocut 2011

200 x 300 mm

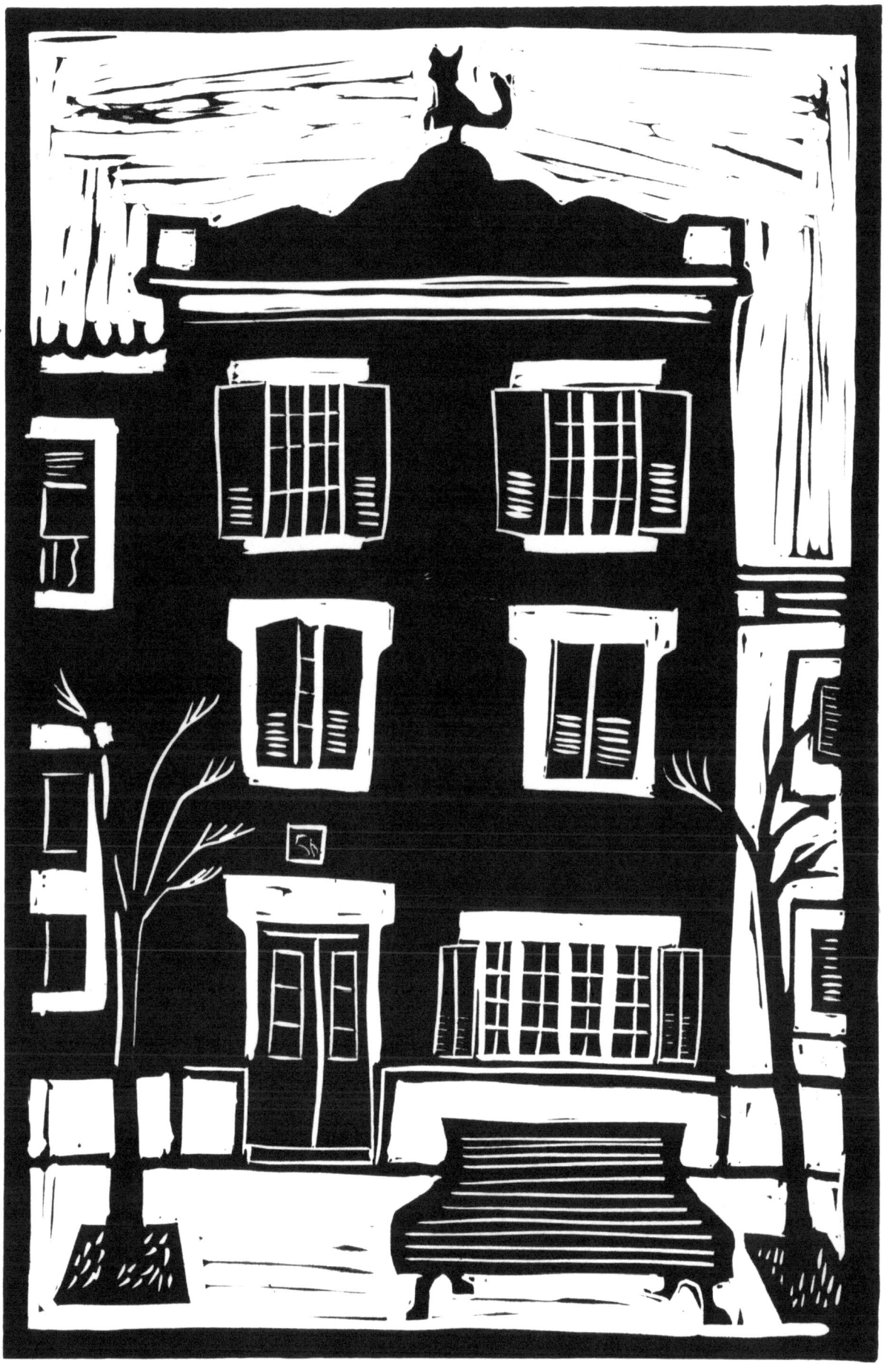

Water's Edge

64 Carrer Bellavista

Linocut 2011

200 x 300 mm

Prints by Simon Bor

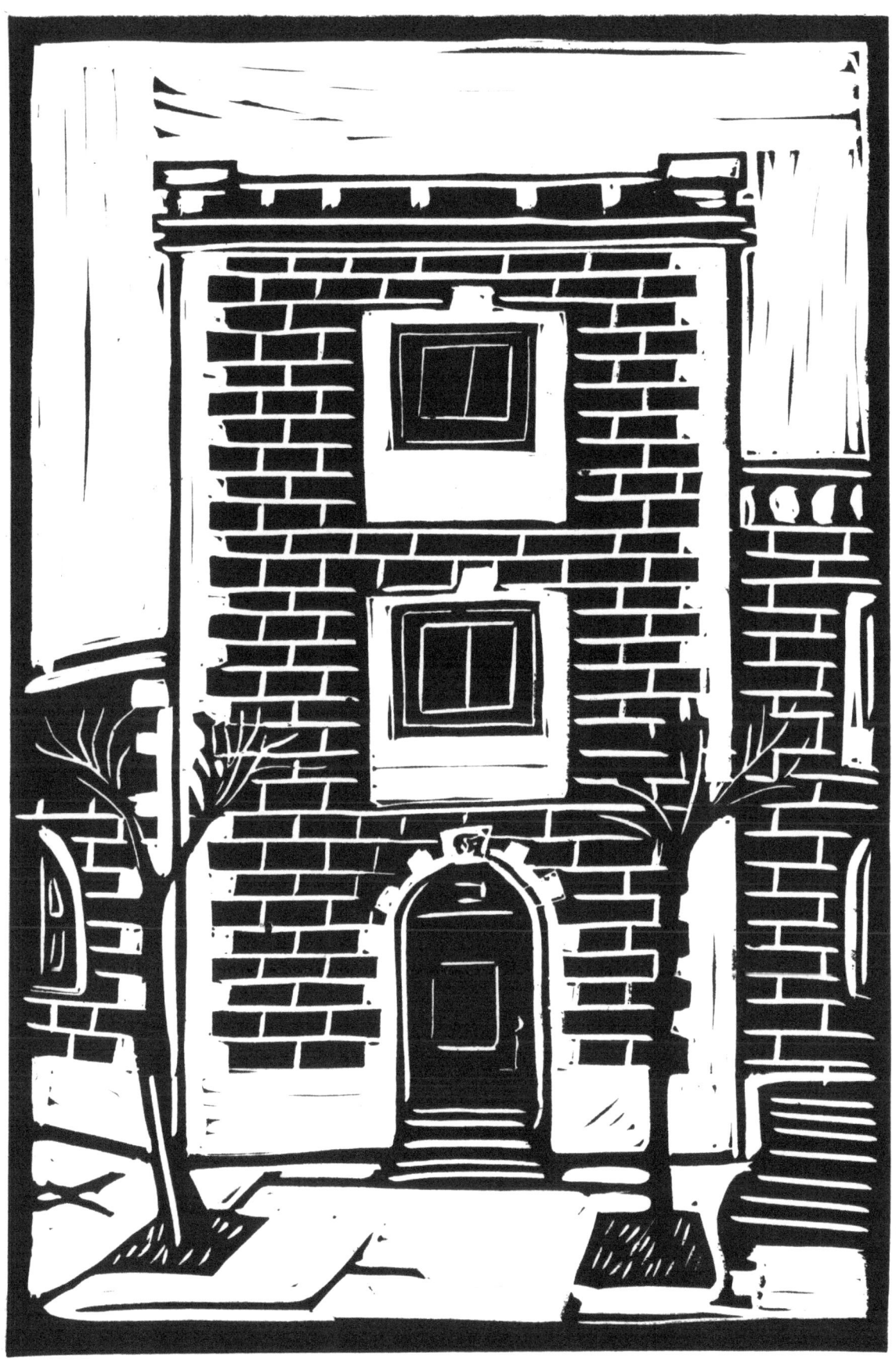

Water's Edge

34 Carrer Bellavista

Reduction woodcut 2011

225 x 300 mm

Prints by Simon Bor

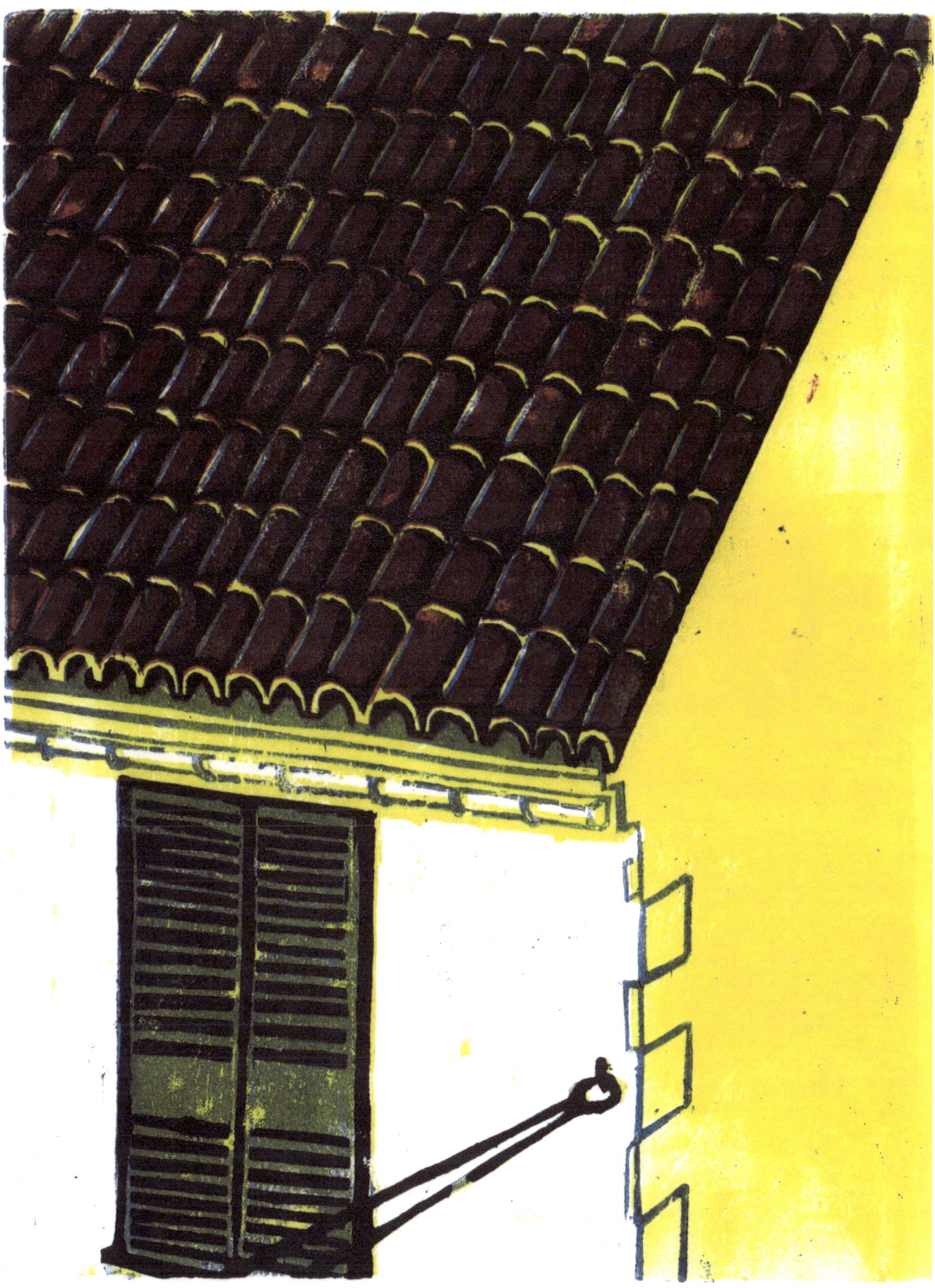

Water's Edge

London

After foundation, I spent a year at St Martin's School of Art, where I continued to print. We were sent to draw on the Regent Canal and at the Thames near St. Paul's. Some of the work I did at that time was used as a basis for my more recent printmaking.

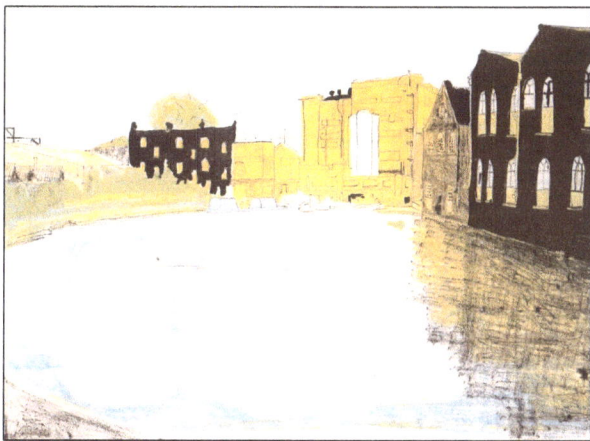 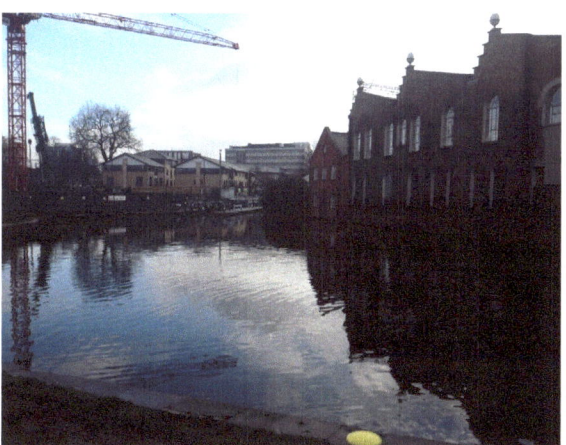

Above, a lithograph of Camden Lock produced at St Martin in 1976 and the same view today. The bread factory was pulled down in the early eighties. Below, St Paul's was one of the locations used in our first ITV series: Tube Mice (1988).

I transferred to Farnham's Animation course for my final two years at college and returned to live in London soon after. Sara and I set up our first studio in the Smithfeild area, long before it became the trendy place to be, and a successful career in children's television followed.

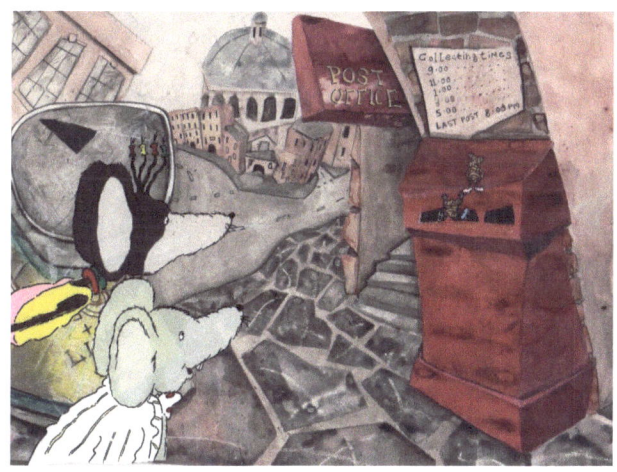

Aerated Bread Company: Camden

Linocut 2016

410 x 305 mm

Prints by Simon Bor

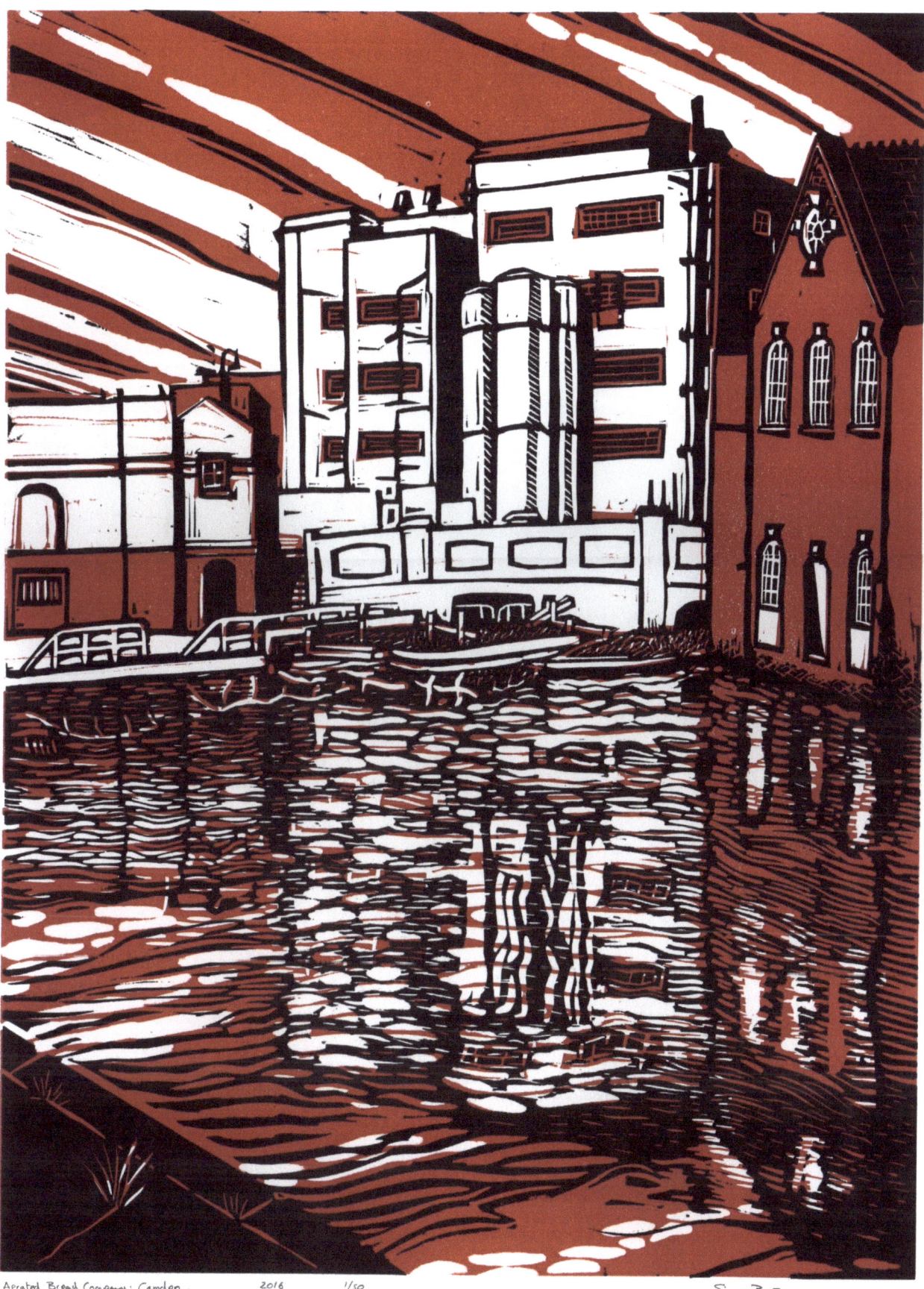

Aerated Bread Company: Camden   2016   1/50   Simon Bor

St Paul's Cathedral

Drypoint 2012

245 x 145 mm

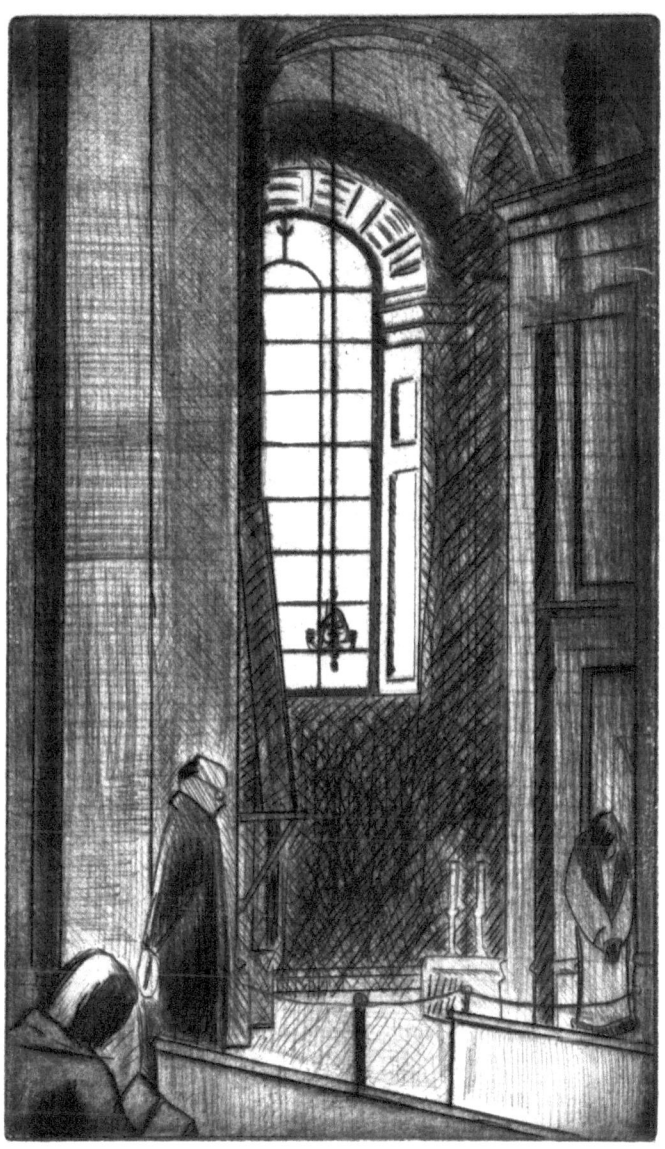

St Paul's Cathedral 1941-2013

(A mash-up between WW2 and the present)

Collagraph and etching 2013

230 x 410 mm

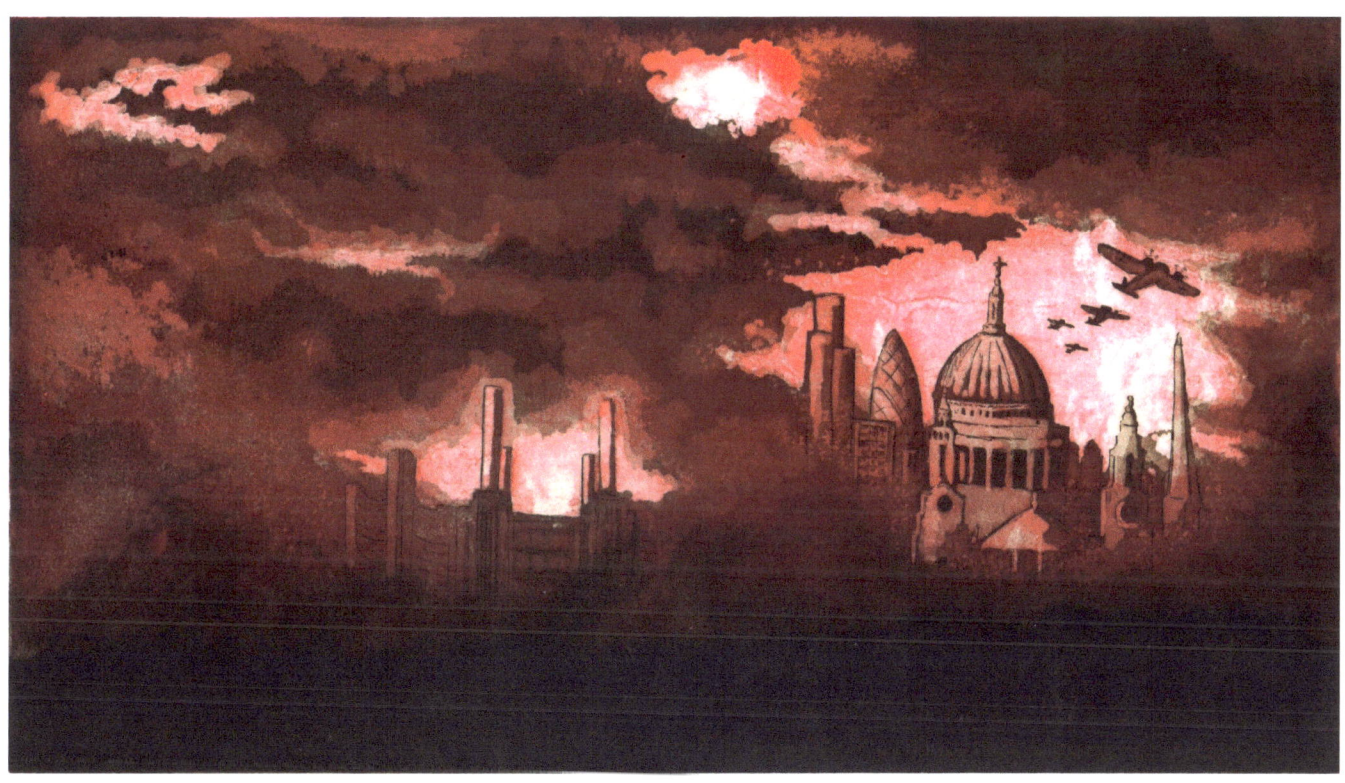

Water's Edge

Argyle

One of my recent prints is Seil Island. As with the Lamorna print, the first colour was printed from a collagraph plate, this time combined with a woodcut.

Water's Edge

Seil Island

Collagraph and woodcut 2017

300 x 220 mm

Prints by Simon Bor

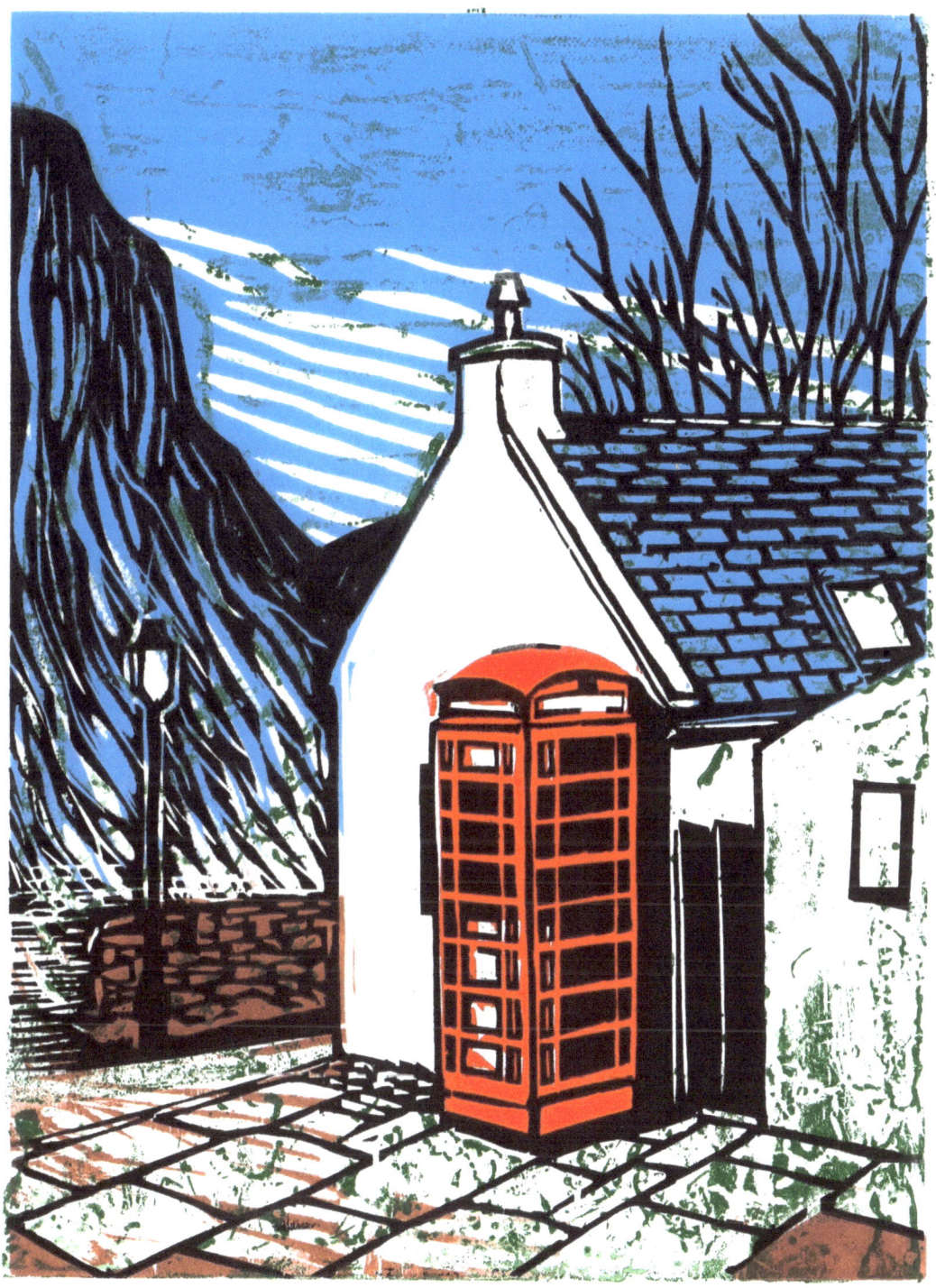

www.ingramcontent.com/pod-product-compliance
Lightning Source LLC
Chambersburg PA
CBHW040450220526
45473CB00004B/1579